ACCULTURATION AND THE CRIMINAL JUSTICE SYSTEM

Dr. Willie Roy Cameron

authorHOUSE®

AuthorHouse™
1663 Liberty Drive
Bloomington, IN 47403
www.authorhouse.com
Phone: 1 (800) 839-8640

Published by AuthorHouse 08/21/2015

ISBN: 978-1-5049-2881-6 (sc)
ISBN: 978-1-5049-2880-9 (e)

Library of Congress Control Number: 2015912928

Print information available on the last page.

Any people depicted in stock imagery provided by Thinkstock are models, and such images are being used for illustrative purposes only. Certain stock imagery © Thinkstock.

This book is printed on acid-free paper.

ABSTRACT

This book provides a somewhat detailed analysis of problems pertaining to acculturation. It is a self-help book that can assist all people in coping in a healthy manner to a consistently changing world. The concepts of healthy and unhealthy acculturation will be processed and conceptualized in this book. Within the concept of unhealthy acculturation negative systematic involvement will be processed.

CONTENTS

ACCULTURATION
AND
HEALTHY DEVELOPMENT

INTRODUCTION

This part of the introduction will pertain a somewhat brief but detailed introduction to me as a person, my experiences, and educational background. After finishing high school in 1982, I attended Alcorn State University in Mississippi on a football scholarship. After playing football for the first 2 to 3 years of my academic career, I decided to get serious about education. In order to get serious about my educational goals, I knew that transferring to another university where I did not know anybody was something that must be done. I ended up transferring to The University of Southern Mississippi (U.S.M) and managed to graduate with a B. S. in Criminal Justice; consequently, I joined the Hattiesburg Mississippi Police Department in 1990. In 1991, I applied for and was accepted in graduate school at U.S.M. in Criminal Justice. I continued to work as a police officer until completing my M.S. in 1993. I had 3 years of law-enforcement experience and a Master's Degree in the field of Criminal Justice when I applied for a promotion within the Hattiesburg Mississippi Police Department. I was not promoted for reasons unknown and thus applied for the doctoral program in School Psychology at the University of Southern Mississippi. I later obtained an M.A. in School Psychology and in 2001 obtained a doctoral degree in Experimental Psychology.

During the time I was working on my dissertation, I accepted a job with the Federal Bureau of Prisons; consequently, my hiring date was 1999 and I completed my doctoral degree in 2001. For 2 years, I had to drive 12 hours round trip from Atlanta, Georgia to Hattiesburg, Mississippi in order to complete my dissertation. While working for the Federal Bureau of Prisons, I decided to obtain a graduate degree in Counseling. This was a weekend program; thus, I could work and attend college at the same time. I currently work with the Federal Bureau of Prisons as a substance abuse specialist. I also have a private practice in Georgia as a mental health and substance abuse professional. I decided to share my story about acculturation before starting a conversation about the topic.

Acculturation is a process by which a person from one cultural group adopts the beliefs and practices of the host culture. The dominant theory views acculturation as a linear process. Within this linear perspective, the person who is considered to be a minority moves toward the complete adoption of the customs of the dominant culture and the subsequent relinquishment of their traditional practices. This is not considered to be healthy because most individuals loss a sense of their own identify in order to fit in; consequently, the word sell-out might be applied to this person. As further research was conducted on acculturation, professionals and lay people were able to redefine their working concept about healthy acculturation. Healthy acculturation is a product of pro-social learning and functioning. The concept of healthy acculturation means maintaining a good balance between your cultural perspectives and those of others.

Mental health professionals and researchers have become keenly aware of the importance of understanding the process of cultural adaptation. Cultural adaptation has been characterized primarily by aspects of contact with and exposure to the mainstream culture. Another aspect related to acculturation is cultural imperialism. Cultural imperialism is promoting the culture or language of one nation. Within this concept, we are all one culture and cater to one understanding of the individual perspective. Cultural imperialism does have some advantages. It promotes the ideals of a collective whole; however, it might represent an extreme view within the cultural rollercoaster. If minorities are forced into cultural imperialism, it might cause even more psychopathology and distrust. The key here is the concept of being forced to change who you are because it might not be correlated with success. The individual who is culturally balanced appears to be more adaptive than those that are on one extreme or the other.

The acculturation process is currently considered to be multidimensional, including physical, psychological, financial, spiritual, social, language, and family adjustment. From a physical perspective, individuals who try to acculturate might appear to present a more acceptable appearance in order to fit in. Psychologically, the person who is going through the acculturation process in a healthy manner appears to be more psychologically in tune with positive mental health. Financially, people who are able to acculturate in a healthy manner seem to be more stable over the long-term. Spiritually and socially, the person who has managed to acculturate in a healthy manner to American society is better able to function. Language is pertinent to individuals who do not speak English.

The common mindset for most people in America is the belief that in order to receive any support from this country you should speak English. So if you are not able to communicate in English, you might not be able to truly acculturate into American society. The process of acculturation can include the family of the individual. Family members who are able to become acculturated might not be accepted within the family that does not view acculturation as that big of an issue. From the physical perspective, the attributions that represent whiteness are considered to be more attractive and less threatening. From a psychological perspective, you feel better about yourself when you are accepted as part of the dominate culture. Other variables of acculturation that require further study include: education, wage, urbanization, settlement patterns, population densities, changes in socialization practices, and pressures to change under the impact of these experiences.

The person who decides to attend college might be considered to be more acculturated than those who do not. Education or the lack of it can be linked to potential or possible employment. Some minorities might have a negative perception about education and think that the individuals who were able to obtain a degree might be sell-outs and only were able to obtain what might be deemed as White or European knowledge. The goals of acculturation were not conceptualized as moving toward any particular culture or value system; consequently, they are considered to be multi-lineal and thus providing many options for the individual to pick from. If the individual chooses to not accept the dominant culture, he or she can separate into their traditional culture or reject both of the cultural life styles. Within the multidimensional perspective pertaining to acculturation, the individual has more than one healthy choice to make. The multidimensional perspectives cause less acculturation stress and probably opens the door for the multicultural option of acculturation. The concept of acculturation stress is correlated with depression and other mental health concerns. It is stress that some people might experience because of not being accepted into the dominate culture or their own culture of origin.

Around the late 1960s, psychologists started exploring acculturation on an individual basis examining the psychological changes that occurred on both a behavioral and cognitive level. In today's diverse and mobile world, a growing number of individuals have accepted more than one culture. Individuals who chose to be involved in more than one culture can be called either bi-culture or multicultural. Individuals who have a bicultural identity tend to talk about their dual cultural heritage in both negative and positive terms. They realize that there are both good and bad elements of any culture. Acculturating immigrants and ethnic minorities have to deal with the question of whether or not to maintain their culture of origin ideals or take on concepts from mainstream aspects. The problem is that we do not know how a person integrates their home culture and the dominate culture together in order to create the dualistic aspect.

Bicultural Identity Integration (BII) is considered to be a framework for investigating individual differences in bicultural identity. Researchers were able to investigate the aspect of cultural frame switching within the concept of developing a bicultural identity.

PERSONALITY AND CULTURE

Personality variables such as neuroticism and openness emerged as precursors of Bicultural Identity Integration. Individuals who are closed to new experiences are more likely to compartmentalize culture. Being open to new experiences which might appear to be negative are important for positive growth to occur. No one wants to have to deal with experiences that could be considered to be negative. We run away from negativity and chase pleasure or what we perceive to be positive. From a cultural perspective, we see these type of behaviors when racism is being addressed. This topic is considered to be a hot spot because it can cause some strong emotions from all sides of the argument. An open discussion about race and racism is what is needed in order to address and resolve this issue; however, issues such as anger, white guilt, shame, and power orientation can occur. Once these negative aspects occur, the discussion can become very stressful and sometimes dangerous. Neurotic individuals who tend to feel vulnerable and anxious are more likely to perceive conflict between their cultural identities and experience stress in the linguistic and intercultural relation domains. These individuals do everything they possibility can in order to decrease their stress level by not talking about issues that cause conflict. Since they function with little conflict interapersonal and also interpersonal problems are not resolved. Other personality variables that play a role in acculturation are agreeableness and extraversion. Agreeable individuals are less likely to report conflict in their intercultural relationships. These individuals are more concerned with being aggreable in order to belong or just to reduce their own stress.

They tend to simply not even report concerns about racism or other cultural related stress and suffer in silence. Any mental health professional will tell you that it is very difficult to change our personalities once it has been established. For the purpose of time, only two personality disorders will be discussed in this section. The first one is paranoid personality disorder. From a minority perspective, a large number of African-American males tend to receive this diagnosis. The person with this disorder will experience severe issues of distrust in a manner that is unhealthy. They may believe that others are attempting to deceive them for their own personal gain. The individuals with this disorder might have unverified doult that lead them to question others about their loyalty. Fears that information will be used against them in a malicious manner and reads hidden meanings in the actions of others. Percieved attacks on their charater that are not obvious by others and has extreme suspicious of others that can not not be verified. An African-American male who perceives that the police is out to get him might receive this diagnosis. From a cultural perspective, these thoughts might be in line with how many African- American males are treated by the criminal justice system. The main problem here is the fact that others might perceive the behavioral examples of police misconduct that are presented by African-American males as folklore that is not true or as an overzealous attempt to demonize police officers. In an effort to address this problem, the critical race theory has been somewhat helpful. The fist goal of this theory is to ascertain how legal aspects are used in order to maintain the social benefits of Whites and also use a power orientation perspective in order to deter people of color. Secondly, the theory helps to address and design intervention and prevention techiques to reduce and or reframe the effects of racism. The problem here is to first admit that a problem does exist. Even current research pertaining to racism within the criminal justice system is not conclusive in reference to proving this perspective.

The second personality disorder to discuss in the section is antisocial personality disorder. One of the major problems that may fit into this criteria is failure to conform to social norms and respect the rights of others. While working in the criminal justice system, I have noticed a small group of individuals who are considered to be (sovereign citizens) but state that they are not a part of our society and the government has no power or authority to punish them. Perhaps this is just an effort to say that "I tried to fit in to American society but could not". This is not to report that all indivduals who consider themselves to be sovereign citizens also have antisocial personality disorder; however, this mindset does correlate with many of the negative qualities displayed by individuals with this disorder. Individuals with this disorder my display behaviors such as lying on a consistent basis and taking advantage of others. They may be experienced by others as implusive and aggressive in nature in order to achieve personal goals. They may present with a reckless disregard for others and a lack of remorse or empathy in respect to other people.

Although in theory any acculturative status can be associated with dysfunctional behavior, research studies have indicated that marginal individuals are more prone to dysfunctional behaviors due to cultural adaptation problems. The personality of the individual who suffers from acculturation stress can either hinder or assist with the ability to manage such stress.

In an attempt to obtain a better understanding of acculturation and the stress related to this construct, psychometric instruments have been designed to provide a concrete analysis of acculturation. The main problem with compartmentalization of such a concept is the fact that now a complicated process is reduced to variables that can be somewhat limited when attempting to develop an understanding of acculturation on an individual basis. Theories related to a unidirectional approach can be very helpful and provide some important information. The major problem within this perspective is the fact that acculturation is viewed as complete assimilation into the dominate culture. Problems with complete assimilation were discussed earlier in this book. However, please understand that some individuals can and have completely assimilated and appear to experience no mental health concerns. Again, we have to explore individual personalities in order to address the differences between the individuals who are able to completely assimilate and those who for some reason can not. In order for unidirectional acculturation to be successful, ethnic minorties would have to be an active participcate in intergenerational awaressess and steps related to direct assimilation. Individuals who give up their ethnic identity and are still not accepted by mainstream society, tend to experience a sense of loss and frustration about not being accepted.

In the bidimensional acculturation model, assimilation occurs when there is little desire to maintain ones culture with a goal to interact with society at large. On the other end, separation is considered to be a method to maintain culture and thus avoid others. This model can also be applied to police officers who separate themselves from individuals who are not involved within the criminal justice field and only acculturates into the professional field. Within this model, balance and experiences are very important. One has to balance the aspects of separation versus developing and maintaining relationships with other people. The interactive acculturation model is more concerned with how the dominate culture responds to specific groups. The first component of the model is related to models adopted for acculturation by immigrants. The second aspect of this model is related to the orientations adopted by the dominate culture in reference to others. The final aspect of this model focuses on interpersonal and intergroup interactions.

The bicultural perspective involves individuals being able to integrate their own culture with aspects of the dominant culture. People with a bicultural orientation have been shown to have greater adaptability than those who assimilate. They also tend to display less behaviors related to psychopathology and maladjustment. Psychopathology is just another name for poor mental health or a person who has a mental disorder. Maladjustment can lead to a mental disorder but if the problems related to maladjustment are addressed earlier enough within the developmental life span of the individual they have a better chance to improve on their quality of life. Depression is often listed as one of the top presenting concerns that minorities struggle with in relations to the concept of acculturation. Problems with acculturation continue today with such concerns as education, economics, and advancements in human lifestyles. Until this point in our society, very little has been done to address acculturation problems. In the past, the individual had to adjust his or her thoughts, behaviors, and lifestyle in order to fit into mainstream society. Criminal behavior is considered to be one side effect of rejecting dominant cultural aspects by some minorities. Perhaps the best method here is to practice the type of acculturation style that is a fit for your personality.

INSTITUTIONAL EFFORTS IN ACCULTURATION

By assisting the person on how to acculturate in a healthy manner and adjust to systemic problems, we can improve on the mental health of the individual. It can take systematic change years to occur; therefore, professionals should focus a fair amount of effort on assisting the individual with healthy acculturation. Professionals should still promote systematic change by conducting workshops and other educational opportunities to assist other professionals in working with people who are experiencing acculturation problems. The American Psychological Association was one of the leading forces behind the multicultural approach. They supported this approach on a couple of different fronts: get more minorities involved in graduate programs in the field of psychology and other fields in the social sciences and exploring how mentors can assist minorities to achieve within the academic setting. They were also instrumental in requiring that cultural diversity courses be taught to graduate students in the field of psychology. Because of the psychological, behavioral, and environmental dynamics associated with this problem, the verdict is still out as far as how successful this project has been or will be. Other attempts to address acculturation problems have been to raise awareness of differences within groups. This is where the concept of internalized racism can be addressed. Over time the relationship between minorities has become stress because of thoughts related to unfair treatment and perhaps some form of resentment. The participants of this conflict can include all people who struggle with acceptance and life advancement.

Institutional efforts to address acculturation should be extended to the home and community environment. Early prevention and intervention practices have to be established in order to resolve this problem.

When addressing community acculturation, we also have to include elements related to family issues. Organizations within all communities have to be able to assist individual family members with healthy acculturation. More importantly, family members have to be educated about best methods of acculturation that will assist with and reduce stress.

ACCULTURATION PROBLEMS

For generations, people have been coming to the United States from countries all around the world. Despite our rapidly diversifying population, relatively few resources have been put forth to address the specific needs of the immigrant population. Central to addressing immigrant needs is an accurate understanding of how acculturative forces can shape the health of immigrant families and subsequent generations. Acculturation gaps have been hypothesized to increase intergenerational family conflict. Intergenerational family conflict is defined as the conflict resulting from typical generational gap across time and aspects related to first versus second generational problems. Intergenerational family conflict, in turn, leads to greater distress for children and parents. The parent and child acculturation gap within poor families are independently associated with depressive symptoms.

The concept of identity is paramount in the developmental field. In the field of psychology, the aspect of identity is related to self-image and self-esteem. Self-efficacy is also paramount pertaining to self-identity. The individual develops an ideal of self from experiences with significant others included within his or her developmental history. The concept of racial/ethnic identity is paramount in developmental research.

This concept is also suggested to be paramount when analyzing the personality and assessment literature. Racial identity is believed to occur on a continuum. On the more positive end of this continuum, the individual has a healthy racial identity and is able to function in a pro-social manner in society. On the more negative end of this continuum, the individual might be considered experiencing acculturation problems. Experiences pertaining to cultural situations can serve to either hinder or assist the individual with trust or mistrust. The influences of history for minority individuals could lead to a lack of trust that might be represented as a personality trait. Oppression and other behaviors related to these negative experiences can have a profound impact on minorities. Because of oppression, some minorities might develop a responding style that takes on a protective stance when dealing with the dominant culture. This protective stance might serve as a coping mechanism for the individual; however, society might perceive this stance as a personality problem. The individual who is culturally balanced appears to be more adaptive than those that are on one extreme or the other. Recent events have forced society and researchers to fully consider the ways in which various ethnic groups interact.

ASIAN-AMERICANS

Asian-Americans have been elevated to the status of the model minority by the national media and other prominent community leaders. They have also been the target of racism and persistent violence and harassment. Asians-Americans have to learn to live in an environment in which race and racial issues are salient features of their lives. Acculturation stress is a gap between the elderly person and his or her adult children. An earlier definition of acculturation stress was considered a reduction in the health status of individuals. To qualify as acculturation stress, these changes should be related in a systematic way to known features of the acculturation process as experienced by the individual. Acculturation stress is associated with lowered mental health status, feelings of marginality and alienation, heightened psychosomatic symptom level, and identity confusion for some people.

The concept of racial identity has been investigated in correlation with acculturation. Racial identity refers to the quality of one's identification with their racial groups and emphasizes how individuals come to recognize and overcome the psychological and emotional effects of racial oppression. The same schemas will be applied to minorities on a general basis. The racial identity schemas are Conformity, Dissonance, Immersion-Emersion, Internalization, and Integrative Awareness. Conformity is characterized by denial or minimization of the importance of race in society and the racial aspects of oneself, as well as a preference for the standards and norms of white rather than Asian cultures. Dissonance involves a sense of confusion or ambivalence about identifying with Asian- Americans. Immersion-Emersion is the voluntary psychological immersion and idealization of the Asian -American racial group and cultures and a rejection of white standards and values. Internalization involves the capacity to objectively reappraise the strengths and limitations of both Asian and other Americans and their respective cultural socialization. Racial identity schemas mediate the relationship between perceived messages from socio-cultural communicators and racial adjustment. More sophisticated schemas (Immersion-Emersion and Integrated Awareness) tend to be associated with a positive sense of collective self-esteem. On the other hand, less developed schemas (conformity) were associated with negative sense of collective self-esteem for Asian-Americans. Validation from other Asian-Americans appeared to have a positive and healthy impact on racial views. The central racial identity developmental theme of all people of color is to recognize and overcome the psychological manifestations of internalized racism; hence, awareness is critical to the healthy racial adjustment of Asian-Americans. Awareness of both interpersonal and institutional racism was positively related to the stages of Immersion-Emersion.

Law-enforcement personnel of Asian descent have to deal with a variety of concerns. Language can cause a major concern in reference to effective communication. Police officers of Asian descent can serve as translators to other police officers in order to assist citizens with resolving conflict. Some citizens who came to America from their country of birth might fear authority features due to extreme corruption in the country they left. Police officers of Asian descent can serve as an instrument for modeling lawful and ethical behaviors within the law-enforcement field that may assist with establishing a sense of trust within the Asian community. The concept of the model minority might serve as a badge of honor but also as a burden for Asian police officers. If the police officer of Asian descent finds themselves arresting a large amount of Asian citizens than the model minority concept might cause some distress and cognitive dissonance. Asians and Asians Americans are two different terms and the really important point to be made here is that not all individuals of Asian descent are the same. People included in the racial category include the following: Japanese, Chinese, Koreans, and Filipinos. Even police officers have to be processed through their group of reference and the individual lens by which they view themselves from in order to obtain a detailed understanding about their internal representation of self (thoughts, emotions, and behaviors).

HISPANICS/LATINO ACCULTURATION

The growth of the Hispanic/Latino population provides an ideal opportunity to identify qualities that promote well-being and successful cultural interactions because they are the fasting growing minority group in America. Some acculturation domains have been identified for this population: cultural identity, knowledge, language, and values. Other domains include social affiliation, daily living habits, traditions/culture, communication styles, perceived prejudice and discrimination, and family socialization. English fluency is commonly focused on within this population because it represents a certain level of acculturation. The term Hispanic can be misleading because it does not take into account a large mass of individuals for whatever the reason. The following countries are considered to be relevant in reference to individuals who have Hispanic/Latino connections: Costa Rica, El Salvador, Guatemala, Honduras, Nicaragua, Argentina, and Cuba. Of course, all of the Latin countries were not included within this discussion but we have to take them into account when discussion individuals from a certain country.

Since police officers come from the general population, we again have to look at the world from their perspective. Factors that influence internal interactions of Latino police officers and Latino citizens are: stages of racial development, level of acculturation in both the community and within the field of law-enforcement, and power orientation. The racial identity schemas are Conformity, Dissonance, Immersion-Emersion, Internalization, and Integrative Awareness. There is a belief that officers with a lower representation of racial self-identify are more likely to abuse members of their own culture.

Levels of acculturation can become a problem if the Latino police officer is more acculturated than the citizens that they are policing. As a minority police officer, you have to make a decision to either be a part of the community or apart of the police force. Some officers but not most have the support system that will allow them be part of both worlds. As an officer, the choice that you make might determines your level of acceptance in either world. One problem that a minority law-enforcement officer might have is attempting to provide police services to family members and peers that he or she might have grown up with. Now, the decision might include rejection from the community or a family member because you decided to be a police officer and not a family member and protect them from the criminal justice system. The ability to speak some form of English is important in order to gain information and acquire knowledge and skills that might lead to success. Some Latino police officers have the ability to speak both English and Spanish and thus perform their law-enforcement duties in an effective manner. Hispanic/Latino officers who are not in a healthy status or transition in reference to personal acculturation can also be prone to use of excessive force when policing minorities. It has a direct impact on whether or not the individual can interact within mainstream society. Most individuals who speak only Spanish tend to have problems communicating and getting their basic needs attended to in general. Other acculturation factors include demographic variables like place of birth and amount of time spent in mainstream culture.

African-Americans Acculturation

Racial identity theory seems to explain only some aspects of the acculturation process for African-Americans. As an individual becomes more comfortable with being African –American, one could infer that African-American culture also becomes more attractive. Negative aspects such as internalized racism have to be confronted and addressed in order to increase positive self-concept. The false assumptions that the African- American culture/community is a homogenous one have resulted in inaccurate data and a misunderstanding of the cultural aspects pertaining to acculturation. The concept of the African-American experience can come in many different favors depending on life experiences, education, and family status. Factors of acculturations that should be investigated further include educational level, internalized racism, reaction to perceived racism, identity and formation, experiences with the criminal justice system, and individual perceptions of racism.

In reference to the study of Black racial identify, Dr. William E. Cross, Jr. is considered to be the leading professional within this line of study. Dr. Cross is considered to be an expert in reference to Black racial identity development and was instrumental in developing an identity developmental model for African-American people. The first stage of his model is called pre-encounter. In this stage, the individual has absorbed many of the ideals and concepts that correlate to the dominate and most often white culture. They may be outwardly displaying behaviors related to internalized racism and either actively or passively distancing themselves from other people of color.

African-American police officers who are currently in this stage are most likely to abuse other people of color as well as other African-Americans. They are also most likely to have problems with supervisors who are people of color. These individuals seem to hold Whites in extremely high regard and tend to look down on most if not all people of color. From a criminal behavioral perspective, these individuals are more likely to commit Black on Black crimes more easily because of internalized racism. Perhaps these are the individuals that we hear about and see in the news and represent a small portion of people of color that the majority are judged by.

The second stage of the Cross Model is called encounter. Of course this stage is a result of an encounter with the dominate culture. The encounter stage might represent the awareness of active racism. Depending on the results experienced by the individual at this stage, emotional and psychological problems can result from racism and social rejection. As police officers, individuals in this stage are most likely to isolate themselves from police functions and appear to be distant or reserved. Because of a possible fear of rejection, the individual might display a cognitive schema and behaviors to ensure that they will not be rejected. The third stage in this model is called Immersion/Emersion. In this stage, the individual might tend to be idealistic about their own racial group. As a police officer, this individual might develop an idealistic perception about people of color and view them as only victims of a society. They are committed and loyal to their own social-racial group. The fourth stage of this model is called internalization. In this stage, the person makes a positive commitment to ones own social cultural group and is able to respond objectively to and with members from the dominant culture. The final stage of this module is called integrative awareness. In this stage, the person is able to value not just their social racial group but other minority groups. They are also able to display more global humanistic behaviors. As a police officer, this person is able to be fair to all citizens and is less likely to be abusive to minorities.

African-Americans and other minorities who decided to get involve in a law-enforcement career have to develop a lifestyle that is balanced and thus not be considered to ba a sell-out yet be a competent officer. When faced with the decision to either be a person of color or a police officer, sometimes the confusion between these two roles might cause internal and external conflict. Some officers have to convince themselves that the system is not racist because if you work for it this must mean that you are also a racist. African-Americans and other minorities are constantly called (sell-outs and uncle Toms) because they enforce the laws of society. This type of language coming from another African-American can cause psychological confusion and in some cases psychological and emotional dysfunction. You have to obtain some type of understanding about the background behind such language so it will not cause psychological and emotional concerns.

NATIVE-AMERICAN

Native-Americans face enormous problems: high unemployment rates, a median income only 50% of that of whites, an increase in high school dropout rates, an increase in adolescent suicide rates, high arrest rates, and high rates of drug and alcohol use. Given their overwhelmingly bitter experience in America, it is not unexpected that many Native-Americans view Caucasians with suspicion and even with hostility and anger. Of course, it would be a major mistake to think that Native-Americans represent a homogenous population. The continuum of acculturation can be generally described as (a) traditional, (b) bicultural, or (c) assimilated. Individuals who are traditional tend to accept their traditional Native-American culture and reject the dominate culture. An individual that is bicultural has accepted elements of the dominate culture and has maintained elements of their own traditional culture as a Native-American.

The police officer who is Native-American has a very interesting job especially on a reservation. Most police departments who serve the Indian nation come under the system of self-determination and education assistance act, which provides the authority for tribes to start their own governmental functions. The state of policing in Indian Country is one of high turnover and poor training. Police officers are left to figure out the best method of resolving a problem with little to no training in any certain area.

Because the areas of responsibility can be so profound, it might take days to address concerns related to call for services. Within Indian Country, the police officers have to be concerned with social dysfunction, suicide, homicide, and alcohol related problems. These problems have a strong mental health format; consequently, police officers have to be trained on how to best manage citizens experiencing these types of dysfunctions and not just arrest them. A mental health/ substance abuse referral process would be instrumental in order to address these problems. One major problem here is the fact that some officers who work for police departments may not be operating in a manner that best serves the local community. The concept of self-governance is important in order to provide the best possible services to the local tribe. The problem is the fact that the concerns of both the tribe and the police department have to be met in order for this concept to work within the field of law-enforcement.

Policing in Indian Country can be dangerous because of the lack of manpower and proper backup. Officers have to respond to extremely dangerous situations with very little assistance. In the smaller police departments where there is only two to 3 officers, it can be very difficult to maintain 24/7 coverage and the reality might be that from time to time the area in question might not have any police coverage. Medium sized departments with between 10 to 50 officers tend to fair much better than those with 2 to 3 officers. The departments with 50 plus officers of course tend to provide better coverage but might suffer from poor organizational skills. In reality, no matter the size of the department most officers have to take on multiple roles within the department including administrative duties. In the smaller departments, specialized units such as the following might not be possible: gang, substance abuse (DUI), and domestic violence units.

Despite popular beliefs, not all Indian Country police departments have Native-American representation and most are not members of the tribe that they police. This can be both a positive and negative aspect because you do not have to be torn between your tribe and law-enforcement duties. On the other hand, you might not have any psychological connections to the culture or the traditions of the tribe that you police. The question to be answered is how does policing fit into the tribal rules and laws in order to create a better relationship between the tribe and the local police department? This is the same question that needs to be answered in police department across the nation; thus, it is not just a problem on the reservation. Research in this area of study shows that when the following elements are present within police departments in Indian Country they are more likely to be successful: strong tribal culture, tribal control over police efforts, support of a reasonable budget, and accountability for services provided.

CURRENT PROBLEMS

In 2013, the trail of George Zimmerman was conducted because he was accused of killing an unarmed 17 year old African-American male named Trayvon Martin. The verdict of not guilty that was rendered on George Zimmerman for killing Trayvon Martin; consequently, we have to attend to the perceived injustice that appears to exist within the criminal justice system. It appeared that such problems reached a peak with the Michael Brown incident in Ferguson, Missouri. The Brown case was interesting because this young man was caught on tape displaying aggressive behaviors towards a store clerk hours before he was shot and killed by a local police officer. The officer reported that he was in fear of his life and had to use deadly force in order to control the situation. Also in 2014, Eric Garner was killed by officers who applied an illegal restraint procedure. Before the Garner situation and after the Brown killing, the problem was supposed to be resolved by the usage of body cameras by law-enforcement officers. This incident was caught on tape in which Mr. Garner stated, "I can't breath"; however, the grand jury did not indict. A story that was somewhat lost in 2014 was a 12 year old boy (Tamir Rice) killed by officers of the Cleveland Police Department. This young man was seen on tape and by others pointing a toy gun at citizens. The boy was sitting down when a patrol car approached and ordered him to drop the gun. The boy pointed the gun at the police officers and they shot him. These situations are but only one side of an argument pertaining to not just police brutality but to unfair treatment. The complete argument will be presented in a later book in reference to the negative interactions that have been occurring between minorities and law-enforcement personnel.

This is not an entirely new issues, I entered the law-enforcement profession in 1990 and had to deal with the same problems. The reality is that most of the police officers in the United States are Caucasian males and most of the perceived suspects in the communities are minority males. This creates a very stressful interaction that can lead to aggressive language and behaviors. For years, this has been a very problematic situation that even today there appears to be no solution to resolve this problem. Perhaps the only resolution is to admit that there is a problem and thus take progressive and assertive steps to resolve it. The danger is that fact that law-enforcement personnel are given the power to take life. This is a supreme power that should not be taken lightly and should also be guarded.

One major concern in reference to the criminal justice system is the presenting question of whether or not it is based on institutional racism. There are basically three components of the system, which includes the adult and juvenile components. They are basically structured the same to include law-enforcement, courts, and corrections. Within the adult system, law-enforcement personnel function to enforce laws, investigate crimes, and to make arrest. Within the juvenile system, they basically do the same but instead of arresting juveniles, they take them into custody. The final aspect of the criminal justice system is corrections. The correctional system is responsible for the action of applied punishment and to correct the person and prepare them for possible return back into the community.

Over the years, both professionals and lay people have presented the perception that the criminal justice system in the United States is based in institutional racism. Racism can be defined as attitudes, behaviors, and perceptions that are allocated to individuals simply because of their racial category. The three elements of racism include the following: prejudice, ideals related to racism, a rationalization to justify the power orientation aspects related to superiority of the dominate culture. The concept of prejudice is simply the behavior of prejudging an individual or a collective group of individuals without a behavioral representation. This can also be done with just one sample behavior from a person belonging to the minority group after which global assumptions are made to include all individuals from this one minority group. Perceptions and ideals related to racism include over generalizations made on a perceptional basis. When these perceptions are not reality based, we develop cognitive errors that can represent schemas that are extended to minorities on a general basis. The concept of power orientation within the concept of race simply means an association made to represent a sense of weakness and strength. For instance, one person thinks that they are strong because they are a member of the dominate race and you are weak because you are a minority. This superiority identity can serve as rational for a belief pertaining to what is called a less than perspective. This perspective states that since you are considered to be inferior, you are and for always will be less than me.

Institutional racism in reference to the criminal justice system pertains to informal or hidden social interactions between law-enforcement personnel and minorities. These interactions are usually negative in nature and end up for the most part in arrest situations and entry into the criminal justice system for the person who is a minority.

Another concept that is related to this construct is officer discretion. Officer discretion is considered to be the personal power of the police officer to arrest a citizen and bring them into the criminal justice system or use an alternative approach to seek justice. At this point, a good discussion point in the book would be to turn your attention to overt versus covert racism. Overt systems of racism can be seen and labeled as such because they are concrete behavioral representations that do not require a great deal of cognitive processing. Most of the research in reference to the criminal justice system and racism focuses on this type of behavior. The problem is the fact that overt racism is rarely displayed and whenever it is presented, the behaviors are shown to a select few who are considered to be safe and who might even hold the same perspectives as the person displaying the unethical behaviors. Covert racism is very hard to pinpoint and requires background information about the parties involved to accurately qualify this type of behavior. This type of behavior looks valid on the surface but requires detailed investigations which most people do not have the time or skills to pinpoint this type of behavior. Both types of behaviors are unethical and can cause serious harm to the perception of fair play; however, because covert racism tends to happen more and is much harder to depict, it might do the most damage to the ideal of fairness.

In order to understand the perspective of institutional racism, we must look at this ideal from an historical context. Myself being an African-American, it is hard to say just get over the entire mindset pertaining to the effects of slavery and Jim Crow. Since most people are still suffering from such negative and inhumane treatment, slavery has to be addressed even years later after it was abolished. Perhaps it was concepts such as slave codes, Jim Crowism, and Willie Lynch that did the most damage. The concepts pertaining to Willie Lynch was to create a slave mentality for generations. Such measures as lynching were used to control the behaviors of people of color in order to reduce aggressive behaviors and overtones. Public hangings were conducted in order to deter possible upraisings. The actual number of hangings is very difficult to measure; however, it was reported that close to 3 to 4 thousand people of color were lynched from the 18th to the 19th hundreds.

Racial stereotyping is done by people in order to make sense of their own personal experiences. Some stereotyping does involve some accurate information about perhaps one to two members of a minority group but certainly not to the entire group at-large. The concept of racial stereotyping is correlated to racial bias which could lead to some officers using excessive force. Because of racial bias and other negative perspectives, the perception exist that there are two justice systems that operate in America. The first one is for whites and the second one is for blacks and other minorities. The system that works for blacks is based on inequalities, poor treatment, and is full of injustices based on racism. However, other professionals believe that the criminal justice system itself is not based on racist ideals and the problem is not systemic.

The pure nature of a system, which includes the criminal justice system is the fact that it does work in reference to the structure. The main problem with this structural approach is that once we add people to the equation; errors are made on a consistent basis. It is the human element that adds errors to any systematic perspective. Some researchers report that part of the system might be tainted but for the most part the system is intact and works fairly well. For the most part any system that has a weak link does not work unless you address what is considered to be the weak link. The two parts to the criminal justice system appear to be formal and informal. The formal system takes into account due process and other procedural behaviors that account for the presentation of a fair and equal system. The informal system does not care about presentation and players in the system can act in an overtly racist manner.

POLICE ENCOUNTERS WITH CITIZENS

Whenever there is a social interaction with another person, we have to be able to account for how prior interactions and experiences may affect our current interactions. It is important to interact with the individual or individuals who you are currently dealing with. During an eight hour shift, the law-enforcement officer might be going from one social interaction to the next one in a matter of minutes. It is difficult not to transfer the negativity from one interaction to the next one especially if the people that you are policing have similar characteristics. In social interactions it is important to take a surface versus background perspective. This background is considered to include the following: prior experiences, emotions, negative interactions related to those experiences, and learned behaviors that are correlated to those prior social interactions.

Prior experiences serve to set a mindset for social interactions and create expectations for behaviors and situations. Most officers experience negative social interactions on a consistent basis. The police are rarely called to deal with pleasant situations; consequently, their presence can be associated with threat and create anxiety for most citizens. These negative experiences are also present for citizens and can also serve to create more negative interactions. For the police, the negative self-talk can include the following: most people of color are criminals, people of color are always trying to get away with crimes and unethical behaviors, people of color are a menace to society, people of color are always complaining about unfair treatment, people of color are just lazy and do not want to work, people of color need to be controlled so good citizens can feel safe.

Some of the negative thoughts that some citizens might have pertaining to the police are: the police are all racist, the police just mess with me because I am a person of color, the criminal justice system is basically set up to hinder people of color, the police is out to kill or lock-up people of color. As one can see, most of the self-talk is considered to be negative and thus can produce anger and other such negative emotions. More importantly, it can produce behaviors that are consistent to the negative self-talk. From these negative thoughts schemas or cognitive references for dealing with all police officers can be developed. These schemas can equal to cognitive errors that hinder accurate interactions and behaviors. From a cognitive perspective, once we respond to a person or a situation through the eyes of cognitive errors, we are not truly responding to that specific person or to that situation. We thus learn through conditioning how to respond to people who most of the time do not look like us. Even if they look like us, they play by a different set of rules. These concepts can create a situation where all individuals involved in these interactions have to become aware of how they process information; consequently, this aspect is called meta-cognition. Analysis of personal thoughts is important in order to become aware of cognitive errors and to also behaviorally change problematic behaviors. Another construct related to schema is meta-emotions. Meta-emotional aspects are being aware of what emotions you might be currently experiencing in the moment. In reference to citizens who have had interactions with law-enforcement personnel even if they have been positive, they might experience the following emotions: anger, fear, and anxiety. However, law-enforcement personnel might experience the following emotions: anxiety, fear, distain, or anger. The important point here is that both parties have a good chance of experiencing negative emotions which most of the time leads to negative behaviors.

A major point of interest to be made is in reference to the environmental backdrop related to negative interactions. Within the law-enforcement community there is a concept called the broken window perspective. Within this perspective, law-enforcement attends to every infraction whether it is minor or major because of the negative environment that the behaviors were displayed and the negative associations attached to the behaviors. Criminal behaviors conducted in low-income areas tend to receive a great deal of attention because of the level of crime that exist within these communities.

In an effort to stop or reduce crimes in these high crime communities, extreme police presence and proactive policing are considered to be a necessary evil. Extreme or active policing has been proven not to work over the long haul and actually might cause more problems. These measures might cause some citizens to present more aggression and negativity in the direction of the police officer. When policing in these extremely negative environments, there appears to be more incidents of police brutality.

According to the research, there appears to be some perceived racism within the criminal justice system in reference to bail, jury selection, and sentencing. However, according to the literature the perceived incidents of racism are canceled out when we look at the role that poverty plays in reference to inferences within the criminal justice system. Individuals with a prior criminal history and are not able to pay money for bail tend not to receive it. In reference to jury selection, some citizens are not included in the process because of perceived lack of intellectual and cognitive abilities. In both of these cases, the individuals who are left out of the equation happen to be African Americans and other people of color.

THEORIES OF RACE AND CRIME

The main theories of interest in this book will focus on social and cultural perspectives. The concept of social disorganization was introduced by W.E.B. Du Bois which reported that most of the crimes displayed by African-Americans were related to the migration from the Southern to the Northern states to escape unfair treatment. People of color were fleeing to the larger cities in the North looking for jobs and advancement and found harsh and profound living conditions. Perhaps a bigger problem was the issues pertaining to cultural implementation. The older African-Americans were not able to make the journey from the Southern to the Northern states and cultural education and norms were lost because no one was able to take on the role of storytelling and teaching pertaining to effective social skills. Because of poor working conditions, violent criminal behaviors, and increased imprisonment of males, the social problems of African-Americans and other minorities in the United States seemed to become worse.

The basics of the cultural conflict theory are represented by what are considered to be conduct or behavioral norms for a certain culture. This conduct is what is expected from the person who is a part of a specific culture and also from people who are not. Conduct norms can be determined by a lack of access to higher education and jobs that pay well. If certain people are not able to obtain proper education and thus get a good paying job than certain behaviors tend to present themselves which might not be legal. These behaviors might include criminal and antisocial behaviors. In my years of working within the correctional system, minorities often report having to commit crimes in order to be a success. Because of different methods of obtaining success for certain individuals, conflict can occur because of different avenues for success. Because of stress related to minority roles, some individuals make a conscious effort to take on a more positive racial identity which might include attempting to take on what are assumed to be European ideals.

Assumptions/Perceptions of the Criminal Justice System

Usually, the first representatives of the criminal justice system in our communities are police officers. Negative perceptions about police officers start early within our development and most of the time are present in later developmental stages. For example, a juvenile might have negative perceptions about law-enforcement personnel that might be consistent even in early adulthood. This cognitive landscape in reference to perceptions about police officers for most minorities is latent with perceived injustices on a consistent basis. This map is correlated to distrust in social situations that are burden with conflict that hinders effective communication. Citizens who experience negative situations with police officers tend to develop negative perceptions pertaining to them. Most of the people who experience negative situations with the local police appear to be people of color. Pleasant interactions with police tend to elicit positive perceptions in reference to police officers. For some people, viewing negative social interactions with police officers can elicit negative perceptions. Our perceptions are based on prior experiences which can also determine our current behaviors. It is very important that our perceptions are based on reality and not on just our subjective experiences.

Perceptions are simple ideas about the world at-large based on how we choose to perceive them. Sensory information is processed and we place information into our systems based on cognitive structures. From a structural perspective, perceptions that are held by law-enforcement personnel can have an absolute threshold. If negative perceptions of minorities are expressed outside of the police community, they might be rejected and the person might be viewed as an outsiders. The same or a similar case can be made about the perceptions that a citizen might have about a police officer. Perceptions include sensations and emotions but are not based solely on them. A cognitive evaluation about an event is the key component in reference to developing a perception about an observed action. A cognitive evaluation involves placing a value of good or bad on the interaction observed. An example of such a situation is observing an incident where a police officer placed an individual under arrest we will say for shoplifting some milk for her baby. The cognitive evaluation about this situation might be that she should not have been arrested for trying to feed her baby. Another cognitive evaluation might be that the lady broke the law and sanctions should be placed on her no matter what the reason was for breaking the law.

We learn to organize sensory data related to such aspects as laws of closure, proximity, similarity, and continuation. In order to obtain a perception about an incident, we have to develop closure about the situation. We reduce our stress by developing thoughts that bring us closure to a situation and thus our perception about the situation is developed. The best method to determine closure about a situation is to just go with the closest perspective about it. For instance, if you see a minority person setting in the back of a patrol car driven by a white male officer the closest perception made is that the suspect was arrested because he is a minority. These perceptions are continued because they can become a part of the systematic perspectives related to how minorities are treated within the criminal justice system.

Race and environment plays an important role in how we perceive the police. It appears that on a consistent basis people of color have a more negative perception about the police then non-minorities. This has been a consistent problem over the years and hinders the ability for minorities to learn how and when to trust police officials. In order to obtain a better understanding about this problem, we must look at the criminal justice system and especially law-enforcement from a historical perspective. This perspective starts shortly after America decided to abolish slavery. During the post-slavery years, the criminal justice system took on the task of supplying cheap and or free labor in order to maintain growth and progress. Local law-enforcement officers would arrest poor and minority citizens for crimes who did not have the resources to defend their due process rights. These people would be sentenced to work off their crimes and some ended up actually working themselves to death. Therefore, because of this history and also current negative interactions with some police officers a serious lack of trust and respect has developed between many minorities and police officers. In reference to environmental concerns, there appears to be an underlining interaction pertaining to negative perceptions especially when the police make contact with some minorities in what are perceived to be high crime areas. Environment can also be a variable when the police observe a person who happens to be a minority in a more affluent neighborhood. Perceptions pertaining to police misconduct can also depend of racial make-up, fear, and environment.

Police misconduct can include the following behaviors: stopping citizens without cause, using force, using abusing language, and other behaviors that do not live up to a high moral standard.

A certain element of police misconduct is stopping minority citizens without cause or what is called probable cause. From this perspective, racial profiling can be considered to be a valuable law-enforcement tool or just another example of a system that is based on institutional racism. Probable cause is a phrase that is used by officials within the criminal justice system in which facts or evidence is present and can provide a reasonable person that an illegal act has been or will be committed. The key within this definition is a reasonable person from the perspective of a police officer. If a person is considered to be a racist, are they still considered to be reasonable? Another question of concern is can a racist person be objective about criminal behaviors in reference to minorities. Probable cause should be based on factual evidence and not just on a cognitive schematic reference related to criminal behaviors.

The next topic of discussion within this area focuses on racial profiling. Racial profiling is considered to be the behavior of deciding on whether or not to engage a person in reference to law-enforcement contact solely based on their race or ethnicity. There is plenty of research within the criminal justice field that supports the ideal that people of color engage in criminal behaviors on a consistent basis. If this research is in fact true than should it be illegal to proactively police minorities? The concept of driving while black became a catch phrase for many citizens who were being racially profiled. From the perspective of many minorities, in reference to racial profiling, the only crime that was committed was just being a person of color who has been labeled as a criminal. Racial profiling has been banned in reference to federal law-enforcement procedures; however, it has not been banned on the local and state level.

Law-enforcement contact can be voluntary or involuntary depending on the situation. Voluntary contact is an interaction with the police that is initiated by the citizen and most of the time they are in the form of call for services. For instance, you called the police because your husband just assaulted you. This example was used because the mindset that most couples have is that the police should never be called in order to address a domestic violence situation; thus, the victim of this type of violence suffers on a consistent basis. Law-enforcement involvement with minorities is rarely voluntary. Most minorities only call the police as a last resort; therefore, when the police are called the situation is usually out of control. The main reason presented for minority citizens not calling for police assistance is the belief that everyone involved in the situation will be arrested. Most minorities do not engage the police; however, the police might consistently engage them. This continual engagement might tend to cause consistent stress and fear of being abused. Perceptions of police misconduct are also correlated with how much ethnic communities are involved in the social and political fabric of positive environmental factors. The political connection of a community depends on who resides in it and how many active community leaders are present. For instance, if a community has a large population of elderly people it appears that more positive interactions might happen between the police and community members. If the community has a large population of young adult males who are not employed, the interactions appear to be more negative in nature. This factor speaks more about conditioning rather than racism. Abusive and disrespectful language by police officers can assist with developing an oppositional stance from most people. What is the operational definition of abuse language? This concept might vary from person to person and might include some cultural references. In terms of racial slurs, we know that this equals abusive language but what about calling a young African-American male a "boy". In a situation where the police officer is much older than the young African-American male, is it abusive language to call him a boy? Where some people might hear a racial slur, others might hear a developmentally accurate term. Sometimes this type of language is in the eyes of the beholder. What is abusive to one person might not be in the eyes of another. This is especially true in reference to the N word. The word in its entirety will not be used in this text because it is inflammatory.

LAW-ENFORCEMENT AND USE OF FORCE

Individuals involved in police work and law-enforcement in the United States have the power to use force in order to entice compliance from citizens. With this power comes a great amount of responsibility that can be correlated to abuse. Depending on who you ask the primary purpose of this agency is to protect and serve the general population. Force and even deadly force can be used in situations whenever the use of such is reasonable and prudent. The question is what is considered to be reasonable in reference to use of force? This question is yet to be answered; however, most people agree that it depends on the situation. Because of the ability to use force, the following concerns are present: the police can and in some cases have inflicted serious harm to citizens, the police can be bias in reference to presentation of forceful behavior, law-enforcement can act in the best interest of powerful others. Even minor force depending on the health of the individual can cause some physical harm.

Aggressive behaviors on the part of law-enforcement personnel can also cause emotional and psychological problems. Some would report that when law-enforcement personnel use unnecessary force the harm is more profound because of holding a position of trust. For many citizens who experience use of force situations, they might experience problems with depression and stress related disorders. According to minorities and other researchers, law-enforcement personnel are more likely to use force against the poor, people who are powerless in the political seen, and minorities. This information can be somewhat confusing because some researchers report no bias in reference to police use of force behaviors based solely on race.

THEORY BASED EXPLANATIONS

Some researchers in this field believe that one major problem with obtaining information is the problem pertaining to the lack of useful theories to explain problems that occur in the criminal justice system. Some theories used to explain the use of force behaviors of law-enforcement personnel include the following: social learning theory, social conflict theory, symbolic interactionism, control balance theory, social ecology theory, minority threat theory, social dominance, and social disorganization theories. According to the research in the field, the literature appears to be mixed. The social learning theory has been applied in order to provide a possible explanation for what is called police misconduct. The concept of misconduct includes the use of force and other criminal and unethical behaviors that might be displayed by law-enforcement personnel. The specific elements of the social learning theory that were applied to understand police misconduct include the following: differential association, definitions, and differential reinforcement.

Differential association is considered to be the weight that is correlated to peer-group approval. Within the law-enforcement community, peer-group can and does have a profound effect on cognitive processing and behavioral responses. Within this culture, most professionals develop an us versus them perspective. You spend most of your time associating with law-enforcement personnel and adjusting to the culture from which you must play a role in or risk possible life threatening situations because you do not fit in. Within this field there also exist a consistent element of danger and behavioral connections to the danger and the environments related to dangerous situations. The reality is that every second that you work on the job, the possibility will forever exist that a time might come when your life will be at risk and you and others will have to respond in a manner to protect self or others. This shared perception of danger is what draws people together because you have to depend on fellow officers sometimes just to make sure that you can operate in a safe manner. Also, law-enforcement are conditioned to believe that they are the best that the population at-large have to offer for this type of job. They are told this in the academy and are consistently conditioned to believe this on a daily basis. Law-enforcement personnel are considered to be the last line of defense against the criminal element. The second element of the social learning perspective is definition. In reference to the law-enforcement subcultural, code and behaviors in the work place takes on a definition of its own. Also the definition of what is considered to be right or wrong can be confused according to the in and out group perspectives. The final aspect of this specific theory in reference to law-enforcement includes the concept of differential reinforcement. The concept of reinforcement includes a reward system that reinforces desired behaviors to increase the chances that the desired behaviors will be presented on a consistent basis. On the other end of the spectrum, punishment of undesired behaviors tends to reduce the chances that the behavior will be presented again. Within the concept of reinforcement, the new officer is allowed to take part in behaviors related to the subculture that either accept or reject the peer-group. Punishments on the other end are considered to be behaviors presented by members of the subculture that lets the individual know that they have not been accepted by the peer-group. In other words, they have not conformed to the status quo. Just imagine being an officer that is new to the department and to the patrol division and not sure if your peers will assist you in a time of need. Within the subculture of the law-enforcement community, there might be multiple peer-groups. Most individuals might choose to take part in the one that best represents their personal concepts, ideals, and perception pertaining to their reality. Sometimes, a certain peer-group might choose you and thus you have to make the decision to become a part of this group or not. Within some peer-groups, use of force and other unethical behaviors might be a way of policing. The opposite might be the trend for another peer-group within the subculture.

The labeling/symbolic interactionism theory has also been applied to explain behaviors in reference to police misconduct. This theory mainly focuses on the subjective reality of the person; thus, our perceptions thus become our reality. If we have the perception that poor people and minorities are all criminals and we should pay close attention to their behaviors, than this is the reality that we attend to and display behaviors to represent these perceptions. Symbols are related to the personal construction of meaning within the work and home setting. The symbol for crime and criminal behaviors might be represented by a young black male walking down the street with his pants hanging below his behind and a red or blue jacket on. Because of this negative symbol, the label of a criminal is placed on the person. Once the label is placed on the person and they become aware of it they might take the label on and thus start acting like a criminal based on their personal understanding of the label. People who work within the criminal justice system such as police officers and other professionals have the work related power to define and also label others as criminals. Another theory used to account for police misconduct and unethical

CONCERNED CITIZENS

When we use what is called the eye test and what is presented in the news media, use of force appears to be a problem especially in reference to use with the minority population. The research is mixed with information that reports that use of force incidents do not happen that much. Minor use of force incidents might not be reported and also if a use of force incident happens but the citizen is arrested or taken into custody than the incident might be overlooked because an arrest was made. In reference to use of force involving grabbing, slight pushing, or shoving, some research report that most use of force usually happen at this level. Again, depending on the citizen these incidents might not even be reported. If you are use to being placed under arrest, than a slight push is considered to be nothing to report. Many researchers report that most use of force incidents happen when officers are attempting to take a suspect into custody and the individual might resist in some manner. In order to place an individual under arrest, there has to be some form of force used even to put cuffs on the suspect. The force can be passive but it is still force just the same.

Further research is needed in the field in order to address the age, gender, and ethnicity of officers. The natural assumption is that young, male, white officers tend to receive more excessive force reports than others. This assumption does not take into account the aspect of internalized racism and the culture that might represent the blue wall perspective. Within the blue wall perspective, race and gender is not an issue and all officers have the same perspectives in relations to policing the perceived criminal element.

In some cases, we have reports of minority officers displaying extreme and harsh behaviors to other minorities within the community in order to fit into the police culture. The job as a police officer from the minority perspective can be very interesting and not a lot of research has addressed this issue. The officer who is a minority is sometimes considered to be an outsider in reference to the police culture and a traitor to people from his or her own community. Early in our history, minority police officers were hired to police only minorities. It was considered forbidden to police members of the local area who were not considered to be minorities.

More research is also needed in reference to citizens experiencing mental health and substance abuse issues. It appears that more force might be considered necessary when dealing with citizens who are under the influence of drugs and alcohol. The fact is that some people who are under the influence of drugs are harmless and tend to put up little resistance. Individuals with mental health concerns also vary in terms of resistance; thus, it is very difficult to conduct research in reference to this population. Perhaps it is the perception of police officers that might be correlated to use of force pertaining to dealing with these types of individuals. More research is needed in reference to the number of officers who tend to use excessive force when dealing with citizens who have a mental problem. Within the literature, in reference to suspect characteristics the following aspects have been explored: race, gender, age, demeanor, social class, and intoxication. The interactional characteristics include the following: weapon, proactive contact, resistance, arrest, other officers present, other citizens present, and conflict. Some other officer characteristics include the following: race, gender, age, experience, and education. Just from my personal experiences as stated earlier the citizens who are minorities, males, and younger tend to be victims of force and perhaps excessive force more often than not. Also, citizens who have a negative attitude and negative responding behaviors also tend to be victims of excessive force. Citizens who resist police actions tend to experience not just force but can also be victims of excessive force. In some of the research, it appeared that the race of the officer might or might not play a role in the use of force or excessive force. Common sense should tell us that whenever a weapon is involved in an incident the use of force by police officers can become a consist reality. The involvement of other officers can serve as a cooling down perspective or be an ignition for excessive force. From my experiences, the presence of a responsible supervisor tends to reduce the chances of excessive force being used. The accepted ideal is that the younger officer tends to use excess force versus older more experience officers. The older more experienced officer might have more training as to how to not get caught using excessive force whereas the younger less experienced officer has not learn these skills as of yet. In reference to education, the thought is that the more educated the officer is the more professional they will be. For the most part this concept tends to hold true but little research is done in reference to the negative aspects pertaining to education and the law-enforcement culture. Some departments require their officers to have at least an undergraduate degree in the social sciences, psychology or criminal justice but still most just require a high school degree with a few years of military service.

The key has to do with the character of the officer and whether or not they will take on the role of a change agent for the department or just allow the status quo to continue. If you decide to be a change agent, then you have to be willing to make some enemies within and out of the local police department.

MINORITY THREAT

Within the minority threat and community accountable concepts, we include a two part conclusion to the problem of police misconduct. Within the minority threat concept, the theme is the belief that minorities represent a social threat to the status quo and the social order of the American life style. Thus, the police serve as the gatekeepers of the status quo and act in the best interest of certain powers to manage the minority threat. One problem in reference to this ideal is the fact that these powerful people cannot be identified. The minority threat and the conflict theory have very similar concepts in reference to powerful others. Because crimes are associated with minorities, fear is also associated with them. Most citizens and even law-enforcement personnel operate through the lens of fear when dealing some if not most minorities. Thus, for the most part cognitive errors are developed about the behaviors of minorities to some degree.

This problem can be compounded by the perceived demeanor and behaviors of some minorities who function through the lens of anger and frustration because of perceived mistreatment. Please understand that my perception is my reality. This negative demeanor serves to further spread the stereotypical ideals of crime and criminality within the minority culture and also fuels the possibility of more negative interactions with law-enforcement personnel. The minority threat concept also suggest that the more minorities one find in one location, the more serious the threat is assumed to be. According to the minority threat perspective, individuals who are minorities suffer from abuse, income inequality, and civil right complaints.

From the community accountability perspective, environmental concerns have to be addressed by the people residing in the communities of concern. Criminals use threat and fear to force individuals within the community to conform. For instance, when a crime happens within some communities and even if you have people who might have seen the incident, they rarely testify or tell the police what happen because of fear. Because of this fear and other problems, individuals from these communities have to deal with the following concerns: social isolation, poverty, depression and a lack of hope, substance abuse and sells, weapon availability, violence, and other social problems. Thus, the so called (good citizens) are caught between the criminal element of the community and the misconduct of some police officers. Most researchers in this area look to the political arena to provide assistance to these poor and high crime communities. The focus is placed on minority government officials; however, the burden should be place on all governmental personnel to provide assistance to communities who cannot help themselves.

Printed in the United States
By Bookmasters